My Barefoot Rank

My Barefoot Rank

David Craig

RESOURCE *Publications* • Eugene, Oregon

MY BAREFOOT RANK

Copyright © 2017 David Craig. All rights reserved. Except for brief quotations in critical publications or reviews, no part of this book may be reproduced in any manner without prior written permission from the publisher. Write: Permissions, Wipf and Stock Publishers, 199 W. 8th Ave., Suite 3, Eugene, OR 97401.

Resource Publications
An Imprint of Wipf and Stock Publishers
199 W. 8th Ave., Suite 3
Eugene, OR 97401

www.wipfandstock.com

PAPERBACK ISBN: 978-1-5326-3316-4
HARDCOVER ISBN: 978-1-5326-3318-8
EBOOK ISBN: 978-1-5326-3317-1

Manufactured in the U.S.A.

Contents

"Francis was so small | 1
We are cars on golden blocks | 2
Fall is here before the leaves know it | 3
It's a thin hand | 4
Silence is old, it's Scandinavian | 5
The notes on my wife's piano pages | 6
Jesuit high get-together | 7
We'd stopped at an alligator farm | 8
Linda says their red eyes are purely ornamental | 9
The 17 year cicadas are out | 11
Dishes in the sink, many times | 12
The Hand that opens flowers | 13
The size of the church always got me | 14
October is the pumpkin's friend | 16
Old people are brave | 18
Aren't you glad someone invented baseball | 19
The speed with which the old | 20
We are not worthy, worms | 21
It's a potter's shed, this poetry place | 22
Mary had a donkey | 23
Why this attraction to old | 24
The bronze soldiers of winter | 25
This cold moon allows for no | 26
Lawrence Welk's Gail and Dale sing | 27
Dark snow, night fields | 28
"It's not about cleverness. It's about life—" | 29
"Landscape with Cattle," by Philipp Peter Roos | 30
Heaven is a large bird bath | 31
In heaven the lemonade stands will be better | 32
This is how it always starts | 33
If I ran things | 34

CONTENTS

Everything was Calvinist yesterday | 35
I want to meet Jesus | 36
Working for mission wages | 37
Not long off the boat | 38
Your ship is not going to come in | 39
The back winter roads in West Virginia | 40
It snowed again last night | 42
Where can we go this morning | 43
The wrong people keep running things | 44
Southwell's "Burning Babe" | 45
Vased twigs spiralled upward | 46
Alberta, you were still teaching us | 47

Notes | 49

"Francis was so small

it was almost like you could hold him
in your hand; all of them—they seemed
to act out their own stories, playing themselves:
feeding the hungry, covering the sick.
But for whose benefit, that's
what I want to know? And who
were the grown ups here anyway?
How were we supposed to take this?

And the crèche, wasn't that the same deal:
life imitating itself? And that little church
he built, so small it could've been stuffed
with dolls or keepsakes? What kind
of lives were these, and why
were these guys so darned accessible?

Were we supposed to shrink down,
fit inside smaller doors; are we supposed
to become some fraction of ourselves?
Would that leave more room for others
in the world? Would we all then come
closer to the part of us that's real?

Is the absurdity of this drama
supposed to make us laugh at ourselves,
recognize ourselves—again. And how
would that experience sustain itself?
In memory perhaps, one we can't escape?"

We are cars on golden blocks

future flowers—a field we haven't come to.

Days there are always what they are:
blue; the sun, colored chalk on the sidewalk.

We'll be finished—but won't be, not really.
There will be so much to fill us in on,
so much of the new; everything but the next day,
dandelion spores discoursing expansively
on the fundamentals of the universe.
There will be smiles from someone you
might have known. Socrates will fill you in,
his life at fifteen—in other words, things will be
just as they are now—only you will hear
what words mean: each loaded, like Keats's fruit;
that ceiling, still as it was in 1821—but transformed.
You'll be able to sit better Steps.

Apples will offer hardier apples,
his chamber music opening as it always has,
into something else—the cross,
which makes everything clear.

Fall is here before the leaves know it

but the foliage has no time for abstractions,
absorbing heat, sequestering, conspiring,
each vestige twisting in the wind.
They scrape against every new name
as they descend, trying to understand
what is happening in the world.

Water is their game, their long epitaph.
Stars are their residence.

Stolid, these trees are libraries, books—
as are the snails, the chained dog next door,
yapping in protest.

They all bow, stand against us, housing
our temporal lives.

This is why we push. This is why we define
ourselves and take their spaces for our own.
This is why we rage through our seven-year skins—
because we don't live here forever, want to.

Each person struggles in a battle he can't win,
sets himself against his planted grass, cuts it
every other Saturday, our angst against what is.

It's a thin hand

that reaches up into the air—
a daughter's, a great grace
that makes its turn above the soil:
just a hand, no rings, no polished nails.

The accompanying voice is quiet,
like the trees.

What Jesus offers is out of time.

If we were saints, none of this would be new.
It would all be kindling: yesterday.
Today would be a canvas—even
the alphabet. You might go anywhere,
take a left and never be heard from again.

Not that the people in that place
would care. There, trellised flowers
find the ground, fresh green.
The world is a sandbox.
Everyone puts out a folding chair
just to watch the sun set. A paintbrush
could make the rounds for years
without ever finding a table.

The world is a large eye—
its blinking moves you to the margins.
This is where you've always lived.

A young woman could live there, too.

Silence is old, it's Scandinavian

snow, the heat of an outdoor sauna—
cigar sweat, good liquor. The nearby rocks
collude; though those farther off
choose to remember when they were space dust,
something fitter than this. But they know, too,
that the earth is good in its way, food aplenty
for the travelling-abouts. The leggeds
don't know where they are going,
but that is their charm.

Clouds are much the same, older.
They sniff the ground like the beasts, tribes.

But rocks! Now they know how to wait!
They settle in the valleys for the long siege,
perch upon ridges, look-outs; they will wait until
only they matter again—things as they should be:
time, that brigand, a passing, futile thing.

Men are like beetles, busying themselves,
fussing, losing all their heat, energy on things
that do not matter, cities that rise like comic hats.
They would do better to bide, to learn
the slow value of the simple phrase, a step
on the mountain. If they could fathom that,
their lives would be changed; they would live
with God, whose voice gives rise
to mottled sunsets, to rifts in oceans, waves.

Those shakings are food for rill and mountain.
They fashion the cold's flakes here—
the whole universe, a vowel half uttered.

The notes on my wife's piano pages

are tiny door stops, mice prints
down a dark hall. I do not live in that house;
no one ever has. Beethoven sits on a plush,
dusty chair, lampshade over his illumined head—
the only bulb under a high ceiling,
distressed molding.

A wolf moon shines on a staircase,
but you cannot live there either.

This is what you must keep: the truth of how little
you are, or, better, of how little there is of you.

(Who would miss that when the time comes?)

And all the measureable world?
Something for science.

Your children, as well: how vain to expect
some stepping off point, where they will find fertile
earth, a perfect mate, though in their noons
it will seem so.

We work in the presence of a God we cannot see—
a night. You can lift your little sailboat,
sail it against a window, the snow outside.

Whatever you can add, I don't want it.
There's nothing else here—too much to take away.

Jesuit high get-together

They'd always seemed to glide
through the good: one an Arch-Bishop!

How have you done this, I want to ask:
prodigals who knew better—never bothering
with what was beyond them?

They'd seemed like shiny Pennies from *Sky King*,
listened to a different channel.

Do their children walk on greener turf, I wonder?
Do their wives, Donna Reeds, still smile bashfully
when they get home in the evenings?

And what would it be like to rouse myself
under that sun, to eat every vegetable on my plate?

Bad life choices are what separate us—
though there is more. My father
walks in me; my mother, too,
eastern European children on noisy streets
generations ago, where no one
could pronounce your name.
They were loud, finding games,
behaving only as well as they had to—
to the envy of no one.

What did we lose when we left them there
on those shores? Whose shoes did we learn to tie?
Though I can't speak for my brothers,
I feel like it's better to eat foods I cannot name
than it is to wave a flag in the country of money.

We'd stopped at an alligator farm

on our honeymoon; and the Everglades,
people circling its eyelid, sunning asphalt.

For me that would be like inviting
arrogant students back into my classroom.
Yes, they have a right to exist—
but not here.

My daughter and I did manage some fun:
the in-laws mobile home community pool,
though we couldn't jump in—pace-makers!

And Haslam's city, a huge bookstore
in St. Pete's, where you could actually handle
new books, turn the clean pages, enjoy
the thick vellum, shiny print. You could
gather a stack, return a few—like in older days.

But I keep coming back to those alligators:
hundreds of hatchlings, one on top of the other
in hungry cages, some finding dogs
or two year olds by now.

They are signs of a sort: welcome to Florida.
We don't have much sense, but our newscasters
are pleasant, and our southern-most
football team wears colors, blue as the sea.

Think of us that way, as sky,
birds over long, bay bridges,
as Chamber of Commerce signing hands—
any name you'd like.

Linda says their red eyes are purely ornamental

these blind urges: 17 year cicadas.
They bump into everything but their mates.
A hundred husks sing the widest tree,
and at the base, clogging sidewalks, sewers—
smelly little Passchendaeles.

They could be all I want to become, my chance
of getting there—an order too large
to comprehend, people teeming on every continent.
You can never say "stop" in this world
and expect a favorable response;
our Father, running around,
making hay everywhere.

It's all too much, too many summer leaves;
the sky, too blue, too big, bruises.

IBM comes to mind: all you can hear
are typewriters, clattering, 50's secretaries
running around—like Doris Day. And what kind
of name is that? I mean if you're going
to choose one, which she obviously did.

Kappelhoff! (I checked it on the net.)
Much better. The world was made for Kappelhoffs,
you've got to admit; I mean, look at these bugs,
flying around, big enough for parking meters.

I wish someone would explain it to me:
this world, these insects, the intrusive blue sky.
It's Tuesday, and I still don't know
what I'm doing. Christ is in His heaven,
and here, no doubt as well—directing all these
small airborn Kappelhoffs,
1949 Volkswagon beetles. (All those small horns!)

Doris got her name, by the way, from an agent
who liked the way she sang "Day after Day"—
and that was her case, too, through more
than 650 recordings, 20 years of movies,
so American you had to wonder
what the world thought of that oppressive perkiness,
that incessant sun.

She was a happy little Puritan cicada,
even when she wasn't, a commercial,
bumping into everything in those years: trees,
her own face on billboards. She defined us
in some horribly healthy way—is probably
responsible for this poem.

So if I ever win an Oscar, I'm giving her
credit: Ms. Kappelhoff—who sounds,
incidentally, like my third grade teacher.

Let me do that now—since I may never win.
I'd like to thank all the little cicadas,
Kappelhoffs, who made this award possible.

I want to thank them, too, for my James Dean
jean jacket, its shredded cuffs, for my overall scruff.
We live amid so many of them, after all, how
can you remember who you are?

You have to pick up your feet to get through.
You could trample a mother's perfect dream
if you're not careful: Frederick Austerlitz
or somebody like that.

Singing in the rain, that's what the world
asks of us, though that was a different guy.

The 17 year cicadas are out

with those tiny red eyes, yellow-orange
rims on their wings, like souped-up cars.
They land on the porch, feet up in the air,
unable to turn over. None of these guys
would do well at college, bumping here, landing there.
If they were people, they'd come over for dinner,
three at the door—Stooges—all trying
to get through at the same time. They wouldn't
be able to figure spoons.

Our big puppy likes to eat them,
but the other day one had such fizz on our walk,
its upside down wings, working so continuously,
ferociously, that he had to give it up.
(Darwin would have been proud.)

We're all like that, of course, knocking our heads
against something; and when our final error comes,
our feet, too, will find only sky above us—
we'll die, buzzing loudly, waving every baton,
half of France, right there on a sidewalk,
hoping for something: a crinkling in the clouds.

Dishes in the sink, many times

Anything else would be too wide a turn,
a saloon made entirely of silver.

Here, you are as obtuse as a cornflower.

You will be the first breathless student
you meet today at school!

The Hand that opens flowers

opens the hands of men.
God, a small salute in the wind,
a day seed that breathes, rises and falls
with a companionable sea.

This is why we eat at the pale table,
creases still in what might be white cloth.

And since that world is already here,
we walk the road to Bean Town—which is not
Boston, though it might be;
where all the inhabitants know your name.

This design and place is more real than we.
Cargo is cargo in this sunny harbor,
on these ships, flanked by smaller craft.
The sounds on the wharf, the ropes and give,
the men, how long do you think
they have been waiting for you?

So it's no surprise your car starts
this morning, that the heater warms.

People you love are near.

Today will be a series of small tasks,
much like yesterday. All my students
will have names, questions.

The answer is the One who made us;
He is our yoke and the hours we try to fill,
one box in the hold at a time, the troublesome
corners which must be heavily fitted,
the sweat and, finally, the harbor breeze.

There is nothing new here, nothing to see.
Call it the slow filling of praise
that forms us, the sacrifice
which is hardly one at all.

The size of the church always got me

confessionals like dim coves, inlets;
echoes of distant kneelers; the interior height,
plinth and cornice, and just
how would they dust all of that anyway—
before money and the times made us
more earthly vessels?

The 60s never gave much, outside of—
so many people: each needing that space,
some of them even knowing it.

A kid among my betters, nothing much
has changed. I still open the timeless doors,
the only ones with answers. I am no different,
just older, the child, giving way to the man
who owns less than ever, and to whom
fewer days come.

Let me die here at least,
among taller statues, saints who do not forget.

Even my sins are the same.

How vast and crowded this road is, its slight rise;
friends I've not yet recognized.

What will make me who I want to be?
How long must I wait?

I would be Your garden—after the tillage,
the long spring. I would be a sweltering
summer home for bees, and then rain,
a greater heat. I would like to live in
St. Thérèse's five-year-old shoes,
sit with Padre Pio at Mass
until I came out better, all my crutches

hanging on a chapel wall, each member
of my family, someone else.

That would be some place far from here—
this church I almost remember.
And so I always go back to where I start,
the answerless quiet—and then
the dark door, outside into whatever weather,
the one that will help me finish my name.

October is the pumpkin's friend

Who wouldn't like to be him, at home
amid turning leaves, sun, on porch wicker?

October is about endings, the nature
of every acquaintance; when each new encounter
seems fleeting enough to matter.

All our best friends come around
in October, bringing covered dishes, what's left
of the year. Someone spreads a new tablecloth,
another brings a dog. Angels might come,
but that would move the scene into another realm.

And part of us doesn't want that.
Because these people matter, however real.
The stamp is upon us—October.
It sings its song in wasted corn, in water
which seeps everywhere.

People wear more clothes, have more to say
in October. Farm doors get painted.
Everyone pauses to redirect sheep,
which makes the commute a little more difficult.

Hot cocoa makes a comeback.
There's always an old stove to lean on
in October. Fewer people comb their hair—
or bother to shake the last leaf
out of it. Bonfires are good in October.
Fires burn in earnest, need to,
each crackling, snapping off more of the year.

Everybody needs to find family
in October. The gold fish bowl holds
a new slant of light. Our end comes in October,
even when it doesn't. It introduces itself

at a fall ball, in the barn. Even when the pond
ices early, you know the glint will be gone
by afternoon. And if the pumpkins gather faces,
well, so have we; and as October shuts
her cupboard, as the latch on the shed
clicks into place, you walk back toward the house.
You don't own that either, but
if you had a bucket in hand, somehow,
the day would be more complete.

Old people are brave

facing death the way they do.
One thinning voice, then two—
against the oblivious, the theatrical.

It would be nice if jokes were enough.
Think of how many comedians
would be on separate stages:
the noise, deafening—and would there be judges?
Tired angels, with business cards: "Don't call me."

Death is unspectacular.
It's like a friend you can never get rid of,
the popping of an upside down coke cup
on a downtown street some night,
long after the home team has lost.

But what if I want a popsicle or something?
What if my clothes bind? No one
knowing the problem, or how to fix it?

I feel like a character out of Chaucer,
under a tree; I want florins to buy some virtue—.
(In 1400 they knew much more about death,
desperation than we do.)

And so, what's left to us then—satire?

Homelessness.

It's all we have; it's all we've ever had.
Let us both lie down and rise up in it.
Let want count on us to sing its song
in ragged coats, swaying together like Rasputins,
or someone equally deplorable.

Aren't you glad someone invented baseball

Not the way they play it today,
but the way they never did. When no one
had a name in lights, when the game
had to end because it got too dark.
(No one could read the scoreboard.)

I want my life to be like that.
May my last out go quietly into the gloam.
May the evening porch settle of its own accord,
with quiet talk, an old radio. We'll remember
the hits, the dives, the catches,
the inning that didn't end. Older music
will start to play—and then sounds,
the laughter from inside the lit house.
We'll turn in, as they say, later, reluctantly;
the crickets, loud as you listen, as an evening
chill begins to touch your nose,
the slopes of your shoulders.

"Cleats in the corner," you say out loud.
It's a whole new ballgame in here: brighter
lights, higher stakes. There's a new manager
as far as that goes, one you hold dear;
and really, what would you trade for all
of this—the older children, as real as you
can take, with opinions and faces
that need yours, regard.

Other games teach you to gather forces,
but this is where your measure is.

The speed with which the old

move through time is lost on the young:
jowls—pinned back; they grip chairs.

It's not easy, leaning like that,
walkers, planted as pivots—
through an ageless sough of wind, sorrow.

This is why they grow thin: all the effort—
the whine, the debris—the g's.

Think of that next time you play checkers
with the old bird at the home.
You might think him distracted, but, no,
he's holding on.

He is warrior, standing in a hall,
not lost, but busy calculating yaw, trying
to manage drag, pitch. (Furniture flies past,
an overly-talkative niece.)

Take his hand if you dare.

Eventually the body tears away.
He knows this, but will stand, past his end,
cracking his neck, ready, he hopes, to greet the new.

We are not worthy, worms

inching along rotting leaves,
tiny music buds in our ears, no
stopping place to call home.

We are a thousand tiny voices
calling out in the dark, a damp atmosphere—
no stars above (always left
when we should be right).

We long for worthiness, want to guard a gate,
a temple somewhere!

But we are tiny: that is our name—
a huge eating disorder, munching alone,
together, deep under moonlight—
the only muster we can give.

We hang our addresses
around what passes for our necks!

We are like Christ, only smaller,
the children of His Provence.
(We would be French, with berets,
Chateau Rothschilds at our little tables.)

Sing with us.
Thérèse's empty shoes, still by the hearth.
We have failed, failed
in our only quest; we are the sound,
the feel of dirt (ourselves) against
the inching, glide—each non-step,
our only freedom or else despair.

Let it pain us! It's a small enough gift—
underground, where no one else lives.
Oh great God of the universe,
hear us as we move our losses aside.
Let that be our voice, our answer.

It's a potter's shed, this poetry place

The clay changes your hands:
each moving closer to the color
and texture of the other.

Your feet do not need instruction.

You don't sing about there
when you are. You sing about birds,
about how they happen: in bush,
on the ground. The spinning wheel
doesn't take you home—beyond
the crudity of its construction, that is.

But this is where your hands come in,
these other things. They belong
to someone else, as you do.
(Its practice is all you know.)

You hope for the silence, just
the creak of materials; no you, no day,
just the slow and surprising rise,
levitation of a by now
startlingly familiar being—tattered,
bright; his wings,
beginning to expand.

It's the transformation you need—
the life that calls to yours.

You are part of the poor, the flowers
that surround you, a bale of hay.

Mary had a donkey

by the ears once, but apologized.
The empty night, hoof beats owned them;
poverty, as it always had,
running bare-assed down the street.

She tried not to think of her feet.
The cold didn't matter, whatever it brought.
(They were always in the jaws of death
if it came to that—jaws that could not hold.)

She kidded Joseph about the name:
"Arnulfo," "Beryl," "Cade," "Dandre...."
She told him twice she wasn't hungry,
and then, later, again. (He laughed.)
And when the sun came up,
she greeted it largely.

What could her husband do?
He knocked on each door, hands full
of morning. He offered the sounds of birds,
a back to clean muck.

She offered encouragement:
"I didn't like that fellow anyway!"
"His feet were too big."

(Could one have a child on a donkey's back?)

"Look, we have become metaphor!"

And then a door opened, not much,
but bigger came with a smile and a torch,
an "It's cold out here."

Mary knew that this was freedom,
and that freedom has its price.

We are always here for someone else.

Why this attraction to old

center-of-town houses,
dining room shutters—on the inside?
The small calm, perhaps,
a world that has long gone elsewhere.
Pancakes in an old griddle
while someone walks his dog outside
past your close porch. There will be a bookstore
near, a church—a rotary on the kitchen wall.

The modern look is all line,
part of an on-the-go lifestyle.
(I don't want to go anywhere.)
And when I do, I don't
want it to be part of a larger proof.
The sun is enough, and the screen door,
the front with an old hook and eye,
a bad seal against summer days.

Two dogs will keep us nimble, and skies—
well—blue. And though the chores
will get smaller with the years, friends too,
let the end-game be beyond me: the place
we go to when there's nowhere left.
The bright arms of God,
where the grass out front stops
just before you know what's happened.

The bronze soldiers of winter

come out of the trees. They've known the years,
read your house before its wood woke soil.

The cold bronze statues of winter
give meaning to the flakes that fall
on their platforms. Small white answers,
they are as delicate as pressed iron,
the will of a wayward daughter.

Winter does not change.
Its paths have been written.
It lays them down again each year.
(Variation is in the eye of the beholder.)
Even the spacing between blades of grass,
the steps you take to work.

You have been here before,
and that is why the child has followed you—
out of grace; into the self she has become.
She is like Advent, before it got its name.

You can hear that in a small river at night.

As long as the wind holds, the young woman
will be safe. But that is why she came—
for the trouble. She wants to taste it.
(And so you will again.)

This will enrich her, but it comes at a price.
She will suffer. That is not new either.
What matters is who she will become.
This is what you wait for.

This cold moon allows for no

other world. No plants, no silver streams,
just you in white. A purer winter,
it's one that spells your name.
The answers are there, what you can find
of them, in dust so old and fine
that it remembers nothing: little cold stars
at your feet. However you got here,
you don't want to leave.

There are no lies on the moon.
Each print is news. This is a poem for introverts—
who don't want the smarm of friendships,
too easily made, too easily broken.
They want people who don't care,
who see others as a new day—each time.
(They don't know you, don't want to,
nothing beyond the moment, the breathing.)
Let them stay there—on the moon,
inside their helmets.

They do not want what you can bring.
If you can sit by yourself next to them,
that would be good.

They don't want completion.

Each sits on a rock. You can't hear birds there;
you can't hear your fellow man or the circus
of his becoming.

You walk the universe
until you're ready for game shows again.

Lawrence Welk's Gail and Dale sing

"One Toke Over the Line, Sweet Jesus,"
on Youtube, and the old daily Mass crowd
comes to mind, their signs of peace—
the relaxed 60s counter-cultural V.

I doubt they miss the irony.
(Their smiles are soft enough.)

Were they at Woodstock, these Steel Valley
natives; or, more likely, part of Nixon's elect?

Either way, like apples, most people
soften when they hit the ground.

It's almost too bad that the world
has passed them by. It would've found them
fit company at this point: wrinkled long-hairs
in spray-painted Volkswagen vans,
gingerly finding spaces between yellow lines
in the church parking lot.

Dark snow, night fields

as pale saplings, like sticks,
the only signs of life, pass the car.
Nothing happens out here: snaking
wind over crusted, marbled snow.

It's the emptiness of the world that saves us,
because nothing can offer enough,
only answers we can't get—aren't.
We could walk any woods, in any direction.
It wouldn't matter.

Things would be different
if we could actually live in these houses,
buy clothes, lay them out, make a plan.

But no, we are turned away—always.

That's the thirst that owns us.
Let it take my life, until I learn
what hands are for. Let mine be chapped,
lined and grimed as a miner's, let them
know the touch of rags—stubs of teeth,
stumps in snow.

All of us regret what we haven't done.
We do it every day.

"It's not about cleverness. It's about life—

this writing"; which, of course,
immediately defeats the insistence.
And so the moment teaches us both,
as it often does.

It's never been the hallowed halls for me,
the great echoes of those (questionable people)
who have gone before, the giants who limped
as badly as any of us. It's about the bird
in flight: poetry. It's about holding it in your palm
for a moment, that quick flick of the head,
bizarre eyelid cover.

Life teaches all of us, always, in books,
the groundwork, in hallways, classrooms that have
gone before. It's a small garden
God has allowed us, animals intact.

I hope my students grow, as my children do;
and often it happens, though I cannot take credit
for what I do not control. Nice, brief companions,
an opportunity—like the guy on the street
asking directions. We always hope we give
more than that, don't we? I hope my 10 o'clock
is a regular circus—one of those birds.

Oh Great Runner of the show,
may we give You glory in mostly quiet ways,
like the turning of a page, new doors,
spanking new faces in the fall.

"Landscape with Cattle" by Philipp Peter Roos
(for an FUS art display)

Moore's student, Ambrose, lower left, reclines
after a day spent wrestling "The Dumb Ox"—
other recalcitrants. (See their bright horns!)
Free now, they graze in a late afternoon idyll,
made possible under and by the ghostly brick,
mortar of what has gone before, towering,
always near, beyond us—a purer culture, Catholic,
a world that never was, (nor, on this earth,
ever shall be); it is a golden cry, whose source
speaks us so we can have our say.

This is where we live: in what could be,
doing what is ours, to make the world
what it is, again. "Come take us, calm waters,"
we say, wanting, needing to own a peace
we already do. So we paint again and again,
part of the pageant, now a fresh bit of sky
in a blue swath, or in scribbles, cubes elsewhere;
in poems, too, ones which can never quite close
because we don't—each of us at Hopper's diner
with some hash browns and a smear of egg,
what's left of a good night behind us,
listening to the jukebox, trying to figure out
how we're going to pay our rent.

Heaven is a large bird bath

We drink from a small cup,
shake ourselves in sunlight;
it's a day of fat bicycle tires, rattling
old fenders down 1960 streets.

I like the fact that we understand nothing—
it allows for ample horizon! Neighborhoods
as they ought to have been—that were.
(Your mind came after.)

May prayer unmake me,
every retreating step of the way.

I will become the last thing I know!

In heaven the lemonade stands will be better

the cries, less insistent. In heaven
every interested party will have his say, living
and more living. Saints will gather like gunfire
around your decisions, each doing what he or she can.

You are just like them, only with more problems.
They walk around your picnic, sit on the bench
across from you, sometimes not even paying attention.

It doesn't matter. The grand and universal network
has gone on since well before they arrived.
The great book has been opened, pages turned, smudged;
more come in every day.

Don't worry so much, they want to tell us.
Jesus, sweaty among His gears, a blue-collar kind of guy,
doesn't care about your sins. He is elsewhere,
crackling thunder, reminding the remnant
that appearances don't count here.

This is how it always starts

a piece of space dust, and before you know it,
Paris, Edith Piaf—her eyebrows of disdain.

Extend your hand and anything could happen:
hobbits, more spirit made flesh,
every move on earth spelling out something,
which is just another way of saying we matter.
(Not in a major way, granted;
but still, a pie is a pie.)

This, incidentally, is why no one listens to you—.
It would be dangerous, you running around,
a cudgel like that in your hands.

Better to try some flint in a damp corner.
Not with manger straw, but a variant.

If I ran things

every old person would wear a crown, every
kid, learn to clog. It'd be a world
of fat chances, a place for words
like "donnybrook," the Scottish "coo."

Parking meters would be decommissioned—
all that saluting can't be good for anyone.

Fewer planes would take off, more grass
growing on the runways.

CEOs everywhere would wear clown pants,
spend one day a week carrying someone else's child.

I wouldn't change myself, though. I mean
I'd like to, but it's better to start small.
(Your forbearance, readers, has long
been noted. It's more than I deserve.)

You've been like the sound of the refrigerator
door opening, the small shifting of bottles,
condiments; the whole experience telling me
that everything will be alright, fields
will come back, and that though I'm attached
to a rainbow of artificial colors, to hot dogs—
in the end, I just might have to give that up.

Everything was Calvinist yesterday

triumphant, sunny, cold: a snow shovel,
gracing a scraped walk.

But then that kid, rolling back and forth,
over a snow pile in the middle of a street:
I had to pause, beep softly,
just to give him the thumbs-up!

The Christmas crib makes us, white chocolate—
cold enough to snap.

Calvinism, though, the American high ground,
comes back, like a dog, barking
sub-zero weather; in an army of trenched soldiers,
gathering behind the house,
a stutter of frozen breaths.

They love Jesus, these Calvinists,
always manage to be bigger than they are.
They know how to walk with kings, and who
can blame them—all that virtue to be had
in the grabbing?

I want to be like them,
a good three hours a day.

I want to meet Jesus

when I haven't showered yet,
when I itch. I want to meet Him
when I'm peeling off winter socks.
I want to meet Jesus where people usually don't:
in the front seat of my car when I have
to shift to snap the belt. I want to meet Him
in class when I have nothing to say, when
I'm picking up a prescription, driving
my daughter to school. I want to find Jesus
in hot chocolate, in my bed at night
when I'm trying to put the day to rest.
I want to find Him when a priest insults me,
when there's no hiding who I am.
I want to find Jesus in the back pews,
in my past, in the diapers I wore,
those old black and whites. I want to walk
with my dead mother again and get to
know her—whose middle name, I learned
at her funeral, was Ann. I want to survive
Guadalcanal water with dad. I want
to get to know each of my nephews, nieces,
their children.

Perhaps this will help me do that.

Working for mission wages

I can't glean anti-climax
from exotic places like Billy Collins:
a café in Istanbul, no cranes in Nebraska—
always on the other side of somewhere!

So what's left: Walmart, Papa John's?

My kids grow between each poem; my wife too.
Our young dog still steals everything—
can scratch himself, standing up.
(Perhaps we should make a video of that.)

The walls in this early morning dining room
are still yellow, that picture still crooked.

(Give me a moment.)

I wait, go to the One Who Matters.
And the present, now, does not seem so small,
but rather, contains all that has ever been;
all I was, perhaps too much of what I will be.
But if we could change things, would we—
our lives leading us to other people, places?

So we wait, as I bring everything
I am to this house, to my children, my wife.
Let it provide them with a floor, walls:
a small plastered place, where my eldest
can do D&D in the basement with his buds,
where my daughter can study her German
in her room, where our Down's guy can play
with his socks on his bed, use my computer.

We see that it's not the events that matter,
but rather, the infinite time between, a space
for left-overs, the internet, where people
carry on in a largely silent bare foot fall.

Not long off the boat

Spanish nuns in tan habits
walk a kind of line down the county road.
Jude and I beep, wave, and I see
Bill and Molly's daughter, a newb; she's
one of those comfortable enough to flap back.
The Church has come from the corners of Spain!

It's odd. Some of them can't speak English.

But then again, what better way to save America?
First off, don't listen to a word they say.
They never know what they are talking about.
All they can do is profit and boss,
social pogroms, always after the earth's hide
in one way or another.

The nuns, thankfully, cannot hear.

No, there will be no Babylon
once they set things right: no more left
speaking past the right, right speaking past again.
The tan nuns will lead us, and life will be
like walking down a county road
in a foreign country for everybody!

Of course, everything won't be entirely new,
but why would you expect that?

Your ship is not going to come in

or you missed it, all the golden ropes,
the seas which spread out before you
like warm milk and a blanket.

Your mother might have been there
as the water sloshed against the sides, but how
could you know? When it got very dark,
you could pick up stars from the sea, put them
in your pocket. Even your best friend, on deck,
at the ready—sitting quietly on a bench,
he didn't have a word to say.

Everyone spends some time there, under
the creak of rigging. We each need to feel
that we're in the right place—that our step has,
at last, found its print.

Some people call it God's will,
and that may be so.
As for me, I'll just call it a good day.

The back winter roads in West Virginia

the trees, are grey as a field mare.
We see that, too, in her cities, too long
in the service of steel. West Virginia
is involved in a game she's never learned
how to play. She's dirty to grey windows,
the speckled seats of the high school football stadiums.

But what better place to live?
If we can get potable water, our clothes dry,
clean on the line, if we can raise kale
and children; we'll take that over taller cities—
where everyone sits on an edge, where sirens call,
each to each. Give me clean enough,
rooms with a little dirt on the painted floors.

Let me sing to God
while making a tuna-fish sandwich. Weirton,
oh Weirton, here is your throne:
a testimony of red grass, snow, grey hills.

The Ohio cannot name you, and I
would not trade my youth for the dull rains
which wash these mountains, streets—.
They tell me who I am, about who people are:
the simple reasoning behind hand and grasp,
about how necessary the Marathon Gas Station is,
Kroger's, Raggi's Windows. They matter
because Jack, my neighbor, the guy who used
to lend me his pick-up truck to collect back yard dirt,
keys always in it, is slipping into dementia;
because single, wide Jim, on the other side,
still talks Pirates, runs his dogs each Saturday.

Who deserves to have a place here, anywhere?
Who deserves these people—or the ones
in my house, their tears and tribulations,
their bad jokes?

We have statues of Jesus and Mary
on our mantle, say our rustic prayers
when we remember. They do not
recapture our childhood, but they do give us
our kids back—each time, along with
the ravines, the rust, the Coke cans.

We will take that, and you,
your family as well, should they happen along.

It snowed again last night

the first time in a month, and I was struck
by the fluff of it. Delicately crafted, the angle
of each new flake, keenly into the soft next—
it was not cold yet, but it would be.

I wait for metaphor—the anxious
truth for our lives, perhaps: my wife's,
daughter's needs, griefs, (my sons' too).
How attentive we must be—as the fabric
of their psyches threatens. It's like we're asked
to be handy persons.

And it's like that for all of us.

That's the snow part—
how it is, who we have to be; the larger scene:
Someone Else's beauty, concern.

And the cold? Our failures, paltry arc! Still,
what can any of us do? You've got to admit—
it's nice to have a place here,
to have an eye for these things.

Where can we go this morning

where have we not been? To our reader's house—
socks on the floor. Disgraceful!
But maybe there's a little train in the basement,
small puffs of air coming out of the stack
very early in the morning.
Maybe there's an electric guitar in the dark.

These are all the lives we've lived, the doors
never opened. (It's not too late!)
And that's why we're here. Because we need them,
too, the things that didn't happen.

They are why fine pre-dawns still excite us,
why the backyard rocks shone,
early this morning under porch lights, rain—.

You never know what you'll find:
a bog of memory, some corpse
you have to pull clear—sponge off the tar.
The rain will continue to wet your face; the ground,
sink you in its hole. This will be you starting
to become, in some way, others.
The dark arm you hold, the two: yours,
its, becoming one; the skull, extra—then not.

Who would be able to watch this?
Two livers, one with the drink; fingers,
sodden vines, one set becoming the next.
This is a dark resurrection, the dead
rising into the dead. The experience
will make you an echo, a chamber, will give you
resonances, a history. The absent voices
will help you to stop speaking, to become
a listening place, a place of transformation.

No one will know you. No one
will recognize you or what's left of your voice.
This is what happens
when you become something of the good.

The wrong people keep running things

but because we have children, we hope.

How else could we endure gym teachers,
Pandemonium middle school?
What is good, what thou lovest well, Ezra—
was here first!

We are a song that has flowered the ages.

Every parent lines up against what has gone too far
and forever away.

"But no one ever gives a thought about
who's right for this job, do they? Everybody,
a winner, gets a participant badge:
God with that absurd generosity of His.
Your pencils break, scatter. You cannot keep up.
And it's not like you can demand a recount."

Parents, meanwhile, cheer the loudest,
make sidelines; they're giddy enough
to spell the future—with their dreams.

Grandparents now, you can still find them
in tall grass, dancing, sticks high above their heads;
they swing them in unison, touching the ground
over here, doing the same, after a step,
over there. They were never right for this job,
but they don't give a rat's ass about that.
I mean look at them: so self-absorbed!
They are the future, off-key, loud as it's ever been.

Southwell's "Burning Babe"

Who could bear the iron clasp
of that yoke: ten times, the purity of pain,
perfected for its own sake?

We are not so hardy, our times less resolute.
We are caught up in versions of ourselves.
(What can be won when there is so little
that separates us from our scorn?)

Who is penned by peace? Who walks that road?
Who would speak only the truth,
which would be birds surrounding Jesus
on a dewy morn?

It's not Christmas day.
Far past the season, we rage for a wholeness
we do not possess. Lord, make me
your instrument—peace. Let me walk
more slowly than I can, because that Babe
has taken the quiet, made it a white hole,
liquifying, for a moment, steel, surrounding stone,
consuming London's, Jerusalem's air:
everything that is low, serving what is above.

Vased twigs spiral upward

like flames next to Mass;
and in the spaces: Kolbe's face—that calm
in a darkened church window!

I thought of Auschwitz and his room,
the bunker where Nazis scalloped prisoners,
wanted hell loosed—got hymns instead;
and those hallway pictures there, some of the women,
still fetching, though bald, dead soon enough—
who could take his peace, live that?
And so, though I can't follow, I must—
down the halls of my life, each moment,
the last Maximilian ever had.

But why does he calm, make those twigs flames?
What does he want me to see?
Lent: this, its first Sunday?

(Like most, I get these little helps,
but then they are gone—like the small
church school TV room statue. I held it,
worried because I didn't know the symbol:
a saint holding a frond.)

Maximilian, what do you want to say:
"that you will be with me," "that the road
is long for everyone," "that I shouldn't worry,"
"that the end of the journey gets revealed only—
then," "that now is the time for twigs, twine"?

Alberta, you were still teaching us

on the last couch left you:
"They won't let me feed myself"—
wry humor intact.

Our professor: poet, elsewhere by now,
where irony has a home, nuance, no end.
How you must amuse yourselves,
you and your poetic buds, each woodland
choice among so many, stepping over logs,
toadstools in your search for wit, conversation.

The rest of the place can wait; this
you've always known.
Hurry never got anyone anywhere—
even when there was somewhere to go!

You don't have to pause for us,
though it would be nice to see you again,
hear your poems as they should be heard.

Linda, as you know, sends her love.

(In bed at night, we are so little, vulnerable—
in God's hands, incapable of anything,
a couple of mice.

Pray that we stay that way.)

Notes

"Francis was so small

The whole poem is an outsider's take on the first Franciscan friars.

We are cars on golden blocks

Keats died near the Spanish Steps in Rome in 1821. The ceiling in the museum room is the same as it was at the time of his passing.

Jesuit high get-together

The Archbishop is Timothy Broglio, who sat across from me in a ninth grade class. (Apparently I did him some good.)

Penny was a typical Puritan 50s-60s do-gooder in the TV series *Sky King*. (She was Sky's daughter.)

Donna Reed was the perfect wife in the movie *It's a Wonderful Life*.

Linda says their red eyes are purely ornamental

Frederick Austerlitz is Fred Astaire's original name.

The last reference is to Gene Kelley.

Old people are brave

The Canterbury Tale here is "The Pardoner."

"Deplorables" here does not refer to Hillary or Bill Clinton. Nor does it refer to Chelsea or to any of their pets.

If I ran things

"Coo" is a Scottish word for "Cow."

Working for mission wages

D&D is Dungeons and Dragons, an excellent roll-playing game for would-be fantasy writers: world building!

Not long off the boat

The nuns cannot hear is a lift from a King Crimson song: "I Talk to the Wind."

The wrong people keep running things

Pandemonium is Milton's city in hell, where it's middle school all the time.

Ezra is Ezra Pound, whose late cantos find a home in the Old Testament: "What thou lovest well remains."

Vased twigs spiraled upward

Saints who carry palm fronds are, in Catholic lore, martyrs.

Alberta, you were still teaching us

Title refers to Alberta Turner, long-time English Professor and Poetry Writing teacher at Cleveland State University.

www.ingramcontent.com/pod-product-compliance
Lightning Source LLC
Chambersburg PA
CBHW072036060426
42449CB00010BA/2290